Why Do I Do Things Wrong?

CAROLYN NYSTROM

Illustrated by
Wayne A. Hanna

MOODY PRESS
CHICAGO

ISBN: 0-8024-5996-X

Printed in the United States of America

Moody Press, a ministry of the Moody Bible Institute,
is designed for education, evangelization, and
edification. If we may assist you in knowing more about
Christ and the Christian life, please write us without
obligation: Moody Press, c/o MLM, Chicago, Illinois 60610.

In the beginning there was nothing.

But there was God.

Genesis 1; Psalm 148:1-5

And God made everything beautiful.
God made trees, flowers, mountains, oceans,
tiny shells, huge dinosaurs, fluffy clouds
—and angels.
God looked at everything He had made
and said, "It is all good."

Isaiah 14:12-15; 1 Timothy 3:6; 2 Peter 2:4; Jude 6

The angels lived with God in heaven. They were His messengers and helpers. But one angel, named Lucifer, said, "Why should I do what God tells me? I want to be like God myself."

Some of the other angels agreed with Lucifer. They decided they would rather obey Lucifer than God.

God let them disobey Him, but they could no longer be His angels. They had to leave the beautiful place where God lived.

1 Peter 5:8-9

Then Lucifer's name changed to Satan, or the devil. Ever since that time, Satan has worked to turn people against God— even me.

He began with the first man and woman,
Adam and Eve. God had told Adam,
"You may eat from every tree that
I have made except one tree. If you eat fruit
from that tree, you will die."

But Satan did not come to Adam;
he came to Eve. He said, "Did God say you
would die if you ate fruit from that tree?

"Yes," Eve said. "We don't even touch that
tree."

"But you won't die," Satan lied. "That
tree will make you wise so that you will know
all that is good and all that is bad."

Eve thought a moment. She wanted to be
wise.

"Why don't you eat the fruit?" Satan went
on. "You could be like God."

So Eve took fruit from the tree, and
she ate it. She gave some to Adam, and he
ate too.

But Adam and Eve did not become like God. Instead they became sinful like Satan. They had to leave the beautiful place God had made for them. They got tired and sick and hungry. And finally, just as God said, they died.

But first they had children. And their children sinned too. Cain, one of their boys, got angry at his brother Abel. One day Cain killed Abel. Perhaps he then buried him in the ground. "I don't know where my brother is," he lied. "I don't have to take care of my brother."

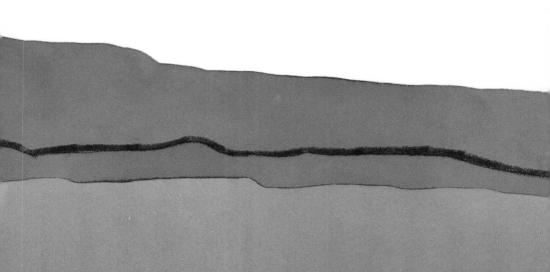

Psalm 51:5; Ephesians 2:1-3

Every person born after that did wrong. People sinned because they were born wanting to do wrong. They sinned because they saw their parents do wrong. And they sinned because Satan tried to make them do wrong—just as he had tempted Adam and Eve.

I do wrong things for the same reasons.

At one time, only one family in the world was even trying to please God. So God sent a flood of water to cover the earth. He saved Noah and his family, however, and many animals in a huge boat.

But almost as soon as the Flood was over, Noah and his family began to do wrong.

And so did everyone after that.

Then Jesus came.

Jesus was different from anyone else who had ever lived. Jesus is God's Son. And Jesus never sinned.

When Jesus was a grown man He went out into the desert alone. Satan came to Him just as he had come to Eve. Three times Satan tried to get Jesus to do wrong. Satan even offered to give Jesus the whole world and everything in it.

But Jesus answered, "No." Jesus chose to obey God, His Father.

Then Satan left Jesus alone, and God sent good angels from heaven to take care of His Son.

Jesus is the only person who never sinned.

Romans 5:12-21

Because of Adam and Eve, everyone sins. But because of Jesus, anyone can ask God to forgive. I can too. And God will. Then God will treat me as if I had never done anything wrong. It's as if God sees only the goodness of Jesus.

But God wants me to try to obey Him. The Bible is full of ways to please God. When Mom or Dad or Suzy reads Bible stories to me, I find out what God wants His people to do. I listen carefully, but I have trouble remembering it all.

So I think about what Jesus said when someone asked, "What is God's one most important rule?"

Jesus answered, "Love the Lord your God more than anything else, and love the people around you as much as you love yourself."

That's a hard rule, but it helps me know when I'm doing wrong.

Once in Sunday school, my teacher was telling the story of Jesus in a storm on the sea. It was an interesting story, but I had a toy car in my pocket, and my friend Bobby was sitting next to me. Instead of listening to the story, we ran the car up and down the table.

Then I thought, *Am I loving my car more than Jesus?*

Another time, Mom asked me to split a
banana with my brother, Seth. I gave Seth
the small piece, and I kept the big one.
  But later I wondered, *Am I loving myself
more than Seth?*

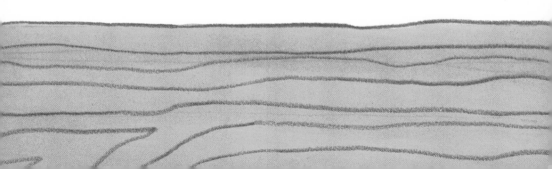

1 John 1:9

But Jesus will forgive me if I ask. Yesterday, Mom went to the store for a few minutes. Just before she left she said, "Jimmy, pick up toys while I'm gone. I want the living room neat when I get back."

But I didn't want to pick up toys. So I watched TV instead.

I felt bad when Mom got home. So did Mom.

Later, when I was alone in bed, I prayed, "Jesus, I'm sorry I didn't obey Mom. Please forgive me." And Jesus did. He always forgives His children when they ask.

Today, I picked up my toys first thing.

Romans 7:14-25; Ephesians 6:10-18; 1 John 4:4

Satan would like to turn me against God just as he did Adam and Eve and just as he tried to do with Jesus. He tries by tempting me with small sins, like playing with cars in Sunday school, or keeping the large part of a banana, or not picking up the toys, or taking Bobby's red ruler because I like it and besides I lost mine.

Even if I try, I can't always keep from doing wrong. But Jesus will help me if I ask Him. Jesus lives inside me, and He is much more powerful than Satan.

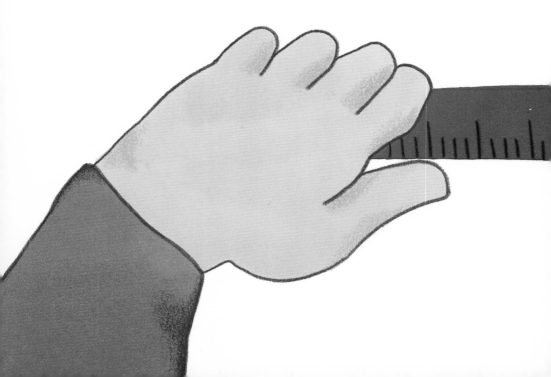

Matthew 25:41; Revelation 20:7-15

But I will not always have to fight against Satan. In the end, God will throw Satan and all the angels and people who followed Satan into a place called hell. And they will be shut away from God forever.

But I don't have to be afraid of hell, because I belong to Jesus. God will take all those in His family to heaven. We will live there forever with Him. Then I will always do what I should do, and I will never again be tempted to sin.

Even now God will help me do right.
The Bible says that God will not let Satan
make me sin.

Last week, my sister, Suzy, borrowed my
favorite book and left it out in the rain. I was
so mad that I wanted to go into Suzy's
room and throw all her books on the floor
and stomp on them.

But I didn't. God helped me say no
to Satan. And pretty soon I wasn't mad
anymore. Later, Suzy used her own money to
buy me a new book.

Ephesians 4:17—5:2

I'm not perfect. As long as I live, I will always do some things wrong. But slowly Jesus is helping me to live more like He did.

I'm glad.